Cajun Fried Chicken Thighs, pg. 65

AIR FRYING

FOR EVERYONE

Delicious and easy meals made in any Air Fryer

 From the Editors at Dash with Catherine-Gail Reinhard & Jenny Dorsey

StoreBound 50 Broad Street, New York, NY 10004

ISBN 978-0-9971012-3-2
Air Frying for Everyone_v11

Printed in China.
10 9 8 7 6 5 4
First Edition

Distributed by StoreBound
50 Broad Street, New York, NY 10004

Executive Director Evan Dash
Executive Editor Catherine-Gail Reinhard
Copy Editor Colin Heasley
Executive Food Editor Jenny Dorsey
Editorial Assistants Isabelle Rabin
Art Director Matthew Pisane
Photography Jenny Dorsey
Staff Photographer Julian Master

Pictured on the Front Cover: Baja Fish Tacos, pg 61

the dash team!

Join the fam! Follow us on instagram for recipes, videos, and daily inspiration @unprocessyourfood

At Dash, we believe that the path to health and wellness starts with cooking at home. From our headquarters in New York City, our team works tirelessly to develop tools that make it easier for you to prepare and enjoy home-cooked meals using natural, unprocessed ingredients.

Our mission is to create products that make it easier to prepare real fast food at home so that you can feel your best. That's what unprocessed living is all about.

Want more great recipes and products to help you cook better, smarter, and faster? Stop by our website, **bydash.com**, to sign up for our newsletter and get the scoop on what's cooking at Dash.

Five Spice Chicken Wings, pg. 29

TABLE OF CONTENTS

Crunchy Mozzarella Balls, pg. 18

INTRODUCTION

We all know that deep fried foods taste delicious but are better left to the occasional indulgence rather than becoming a staple of your diet—at least that's what my scale tells me. So what's a fried-food aficionado to do?

When I need my fix of crispy deliciousness, I turn to Air Frying. Our Dash Air Fryers use hot air to cook without added oil, making them a guilt-free solution to quench my craving for crunchy.

We wrote this book using our Compact Air Fryer and have sized the recipes to fit that appliance. If you're using another brand, you may need to make some adjustments and should refer to your product manual for suggested cooking times.

In Air Frying for Everyone, Jenny and our team of talented recipe developers and test-cooks have created an easy-to-follow guide for getting the most from your Air Fryer. We've found that there's so much you can cook in an Air Fryer that it might surprise even the seasoned home cook. From satisfying entrées like Cajun Fried Chicken Thighs (page 65), to Lemon Shishito Peppers (page 117), to Easy Cinnamon Rolls (page 137).

At Dash, we're all about practical solutions to get you in the kitchen and cooking delicious, unprocessed food. So jump in and experiment—we believe there are no mistakes in cooking, only learning experiences (and believe me, I've had plenty of those).

Happy cooking!

Catherine-Gail Reinhard
Executive Editor, Dash

ALL
ABOUT
AIR FRYING

Everyone loves fried foods. It's that crispy, delicious, crunchy texture and savory flavor that's just irresistible. But what we don't love is the icky, heavy feeling we get after over-indulging in a funnel-cake at the county fair or after scarfing that last fried chicken wing.

Enter the Air Fryer. Using rapid air circulation, the Air Fryer is able to "fry" ingredients without any oil or butter. This preserves delicious flavor and a crispy texture while helping to eliminate extra calories from added oil. Enjoy everything from classic french fries, to fried chicken, to savory spring rolls with your Air Fryer, and that's just the beginning.

Spring Rolls, pg. 45

It's a Dry Heat

An Air Fryer is similar to a convection oven in the principles that it uses to cook. Hot air circulates around the food and creates a crispy layer on the outside. Since the heat is contained in the Basket, some Air Fryers are able to cook faster than a convection oven.

Simple & Healthy

Air Fryers can be used to "fry" everything from appetizers to desserts. To get started, you add your ingredients to the Basket, set the time and temperature and let your Air Fryer do the rest.

Since Air Fryers cook with dry heat, you can also use an Air Fryer to bake and roast. In this book, we have included a wide variety of recipes from meatballs, to tacos, to donuts.

Zero Oil = A Better Way To Fry

From crunchy zucchini fries to buffalo wings, it's hard to believe that this appliance doesn't require any oil. Less oil doesn't only mean less calories, it also means a better cooking experience.

Preparing your food in an Air Fryer is a cleaner way to cook, eliminating the extra parts and added mess that come with deep frying. Air Frying is a convenient way to fry without sacrificing flavor.

Onion Rings, pg. 111

TIPS WHEN AIR FRYING

- Avoid overcrowding the Basket of your Air Fryer. Overcrowding your ingredients will prevent them from getting crispy.

- Opening your Air Fryer to check your ingredients during cooking is okay and will not affect the cooking process. Sometimes with smaller ingredients it is beneficial to shake them halfway through the cooking time to ensure optimal crispy texture. Use the included chart on page 9 to see which foods are recommended for shaking.

- Preheat your Air Fryer to ensure that the ingredients can be placed in the Basket with no waiting time.

- If using oil to coat your food, we recommend using these types of oils; Refined peanut oil, refined grapeseed oil or extra light olive oil

- We recommend using a very small amount of oil, or an oil mister, in order to avoid greasy results.

FREQUENTLY ASKED QUESTIONS

What happens if I use oil?

If you do plan on adding oil to your ingredients, do so sparingly as the results will be significantly richer than expected. Adding oil may turn ingredients greasy, especially ingredients such as frozen french fries which already have some oil. We do encourage everyone to experiment with a wide variety of ingredients, and find new great ways to use your Air Fryer. Adding a small amount of olive oil, or using an oil mister to gently spray the ingredients, can add delicious texture to your recipe. If you find that your recipe turns out greasy, cut back.

How long does it take to air fry different ingredients?

Depending on the size and type of ingredients, your Air Fryer may take a shorter or longer time to fully cook the food. Use the included charts to determine cooking time or refer to the manual that comes with your Air Fryer. You may need to add a few minutes in order to crisp larger ingredients.

Do I prepare ingredients the same way I would if using a deep fryer?

The Air Fryer cooks your food using rapid air circulation that produces crispy, crunchy food like a deep fryer but there are some differences. Liquid-based batters like tempura batter will not work in an Air Fryer. Pre-made frozen appetizers with a crust like chicken fingers will yield an excellent result in your Air Fryer.

Experiment with breading ingredients or simply adding them to the Air Fryer with no extra coating. Your results will be similar to ones using a traditional frying method.

How do I assemble and disassemble my Air Fryer?

Part of why we love this appliance so much has to do with the convenient and safe assembly and disassembly process. Simply plug in your Air Fryer on a stable surface, pull out the Basket, and add your desired ingredients. Slide the drawer back into the Air Fryer, set your temperature, then your time, and that's it!

Does the size of my ingredients affect the results?

Larger ingredients may take longer to cook, and may require a higher temperature. Refer to the recipe and chart guidelines on the following page for exact specifications, however, be aware that these are general measurements and you may have to adjust your time and temperature to fully cook the ingredients. For smaller ingredients, we have found that gently shaking the Basket halfway through the cooking process helps to crisp up ingredients. This will not affect the Air Fryer at all, and will help cook individual foods thoroughly.

What if my food is not crisp when I remove it?

Ensure that you have cooked the food at the proper temperature and for the correct amount of time. It is important to remember that these recommendations are guidelines and that some foods require adjustment when air frying. Frozen foods may take longer to crisp up as well.

Do not place wet ingredients into the Air Fryer, as they will not become crispy. Before air frying, gently pat ingredients dry, such as marinated chicken or vegetables, so they are not too wet before cooking.

If white smoke is emitting from the Air Fryer, this means that the ingredients have more fat or may be too wet. This is not a problem. If you see black smoke, however, this may be a sign that the appliance is malfunctioning. Immediately turn off your Air Fryer and call the manufacturer.

How do I ensure that meat/poultry is properly cooked through?

We recommend using a food thermometer to ensure that these foods are properly done. This chart explains what the inside temperature should be using a meat thermometer.

Recommended Minimum Internal Temperatures for Food Safety

INGREDIENT	TEMPERATURE
Ground beef/pork	160°F
Ground turkey/chicken	165°F
Pork	145°F
Chicken	165°F
Fish	140°F

TIME & TEMPERATURE RECOMMENDATIONS

Keep in mind that these settings are general indications. As ingredients differ in origin, size, shape and brand, we cannot guarantee the best settings for your ingredients. These charts were developed for Dash Compact Air Fryers but if you own a different Air Fryer, you may want to refer to your product manual.

Meat
400°F

Poultry
400°F

Potatoes
350°-400°F

Frozen
390°F

Snacks
320°-390°F

Baking
320°-390°F

AIR FRYER SETTINGS

	MIN-MAX AMOUNT (OZ.)	TIME	TEMPERATURE (°F)	SHAKE	NOTES
POTATOES & FRIES					
Thin Frozen Fries	16-32 oz.	10-16	390°	Shake Twice	
Thick Frozen Fries	16-32 oz.	15-20	390°	Shake Twice	
Homemade Potato Wedges	16-32 oz.	20-25	400°	Shake Twice	Add ½ tsp of oil
Homemade Fries (8x8mm)	16-32 oz.	10-15	400°	Shake Twice	Add ½ tsp of oil
Homemade Potato Cubes	16-32 oz.	12-18	400°	Shake Twice	Add ½ tsp of oil
Rosti	12 oz.	12-18	350°	Shake Twice	
Potato Gratin	26 oz.	15-18	390°	Shake Twice	
MEAT & POULTRY					
Steak	5-26 oz.	20-25	400°		
Pork Chops	5-26 oz.	20-25	400°		
Hamburger	5-26 oz.	20-25	400°		
Sausage Roll	5-26 oz.	20-25	400°		
Drumsticks	5-26 oz.	18-22	400°		
Chicken Breast	5-26 oz.	20-25	400°		
SNACKS					
Spring Rolls	5-21 oz.	10-15	390°	Shake	Use oven-ready
Frozen Chicken Nuggets	5-26 oz.	6-10	390°	Shake	Use oven-ready
Frozen Fish Sticks	5-21 oz.	10	390°		Use oven-ready
Mozzarella Sticks	5-21 oz.	8-10	350°		Use oven-ready
Stuffed Vegetables	5-21 oz.	10	320°		
BAKING					
Cake	16oz.	20-25	320°		Use baking tin
Quiche	21 oz.	20-22	350°		Use baking tin/oven dish
Muffins	16 oz.	15-18	390°		Use baking tin
Sweet Snacks	21 oz.	20	320°		Use baking tin/oven dish

Feta Triangles, pg. 19

APPETIZERS

Temperature: 400ºF   Time: 10 minutes

FIVE SPICE MEATBALLS

INGREDIENTS

1 lb ground pork

1 tsp kosher salt

2 tbsp unsalted, plain breadcrumbs

1 tbsp Chinese 5 spice powder

1 large egg

½ tsp sesame oil

DIRECTIONS

Combine pork, salt, breadcrumbs, 5 spice-powder, sesame oil and egg in large bowl.

Mix together by hand until well combined.

Use hands or scoop to form 1.5" balls and place 6 balls at a time into Air Fryer in one layer.

Fry for 10 minutes.

CRAB RANGOONS

INGREDIENTS

¼ cup crab meat, diced

¼ cup cream cheese, softened

1 tsp kosher salt

1 tsp black pepper

2 tsp scallion, minced

2 tsp cilantro, minced (optional)

⅛ inch ginger, minced (optional)

15-20 rectangular wonton wrappers

1 tbsp vegetable oil

DIRECTIONS

In a medium bowl, combine crab, cream cheese, salt, black pepper, scallion, cilantro and ginger. Mix thoroughly to combine.

Place 2 tsp of mixture in the center of wonton wrapper. Wet all edges of wonton with water and fold diagonally to create a triangle wrapper.

Press down on all edges firmly to seal. Brush rangoons with oil.

Place 4-5 crab rangoons in Air Fryer per batch, in one layer, careful to minimize overlapping. Fry for 10 minutes at 400°F, shaking once halfway through the cooking cycle.

POTATO GRATIN CUPS

INGREDIENTS

2 large potatoes

2 eggs, beaten

6 tbsp coconut cream

1 tbsp all-purpose flour

1 oz cheddar cheese

DIRECTIONS

Slice the potatoes thinly with their skin still on and place them in the Air Fryer and cook them for 10 minutes until crispy.

While they are cooking, prepare the sauce. Mix together two eggs, the coconut cream, and the flour.

Take the potatoes out of the Air Fryer (once they are crispy) and line the bottom of four ramekins. Cover with the cream mixture, sprinkle with the cheese, and cook for another 10 minutes on 390°F.

Temperature: 400ºF   Time: 10 minutes

CRAB CAKES

INGREDIENTS

8 oz lump crab meat, cooked

½ cup unsalted, plain bread crumbs

2 eggs

1 tsp kosher salt

¼ tsp garlic powder

¼ tsp onion powder

½ tsp Cajun seasoning

1 tsp dill, minced

1 tsp parsley, minced

Spicy Mayo

1 tbsp Sriracha

3 tbsp mayonnaise

DIRECTIONS

Combine crab meat, bread crumbs, eggs, salt, garlic powder, onion powder, Cajun seasoning, dill and parsley in bowl and mix thoroughly.

Form into 2" balls and flatten into round discs.

Place 2-3 patties in Air Fryer in one layer and fry for 10 minutes.

Combine Sriracha and mayonnaise and stir to combine. Serve crab cakes with spicy Sriracha mayo and lemon wedges, if desired.

Temperature: 400ºF   Time: 8 minutes

CRUNCHY MOZZARELLA BALLS

INGREDIENTS

16 fresh mozzarella balls (usually marked as "Ciliegine" or cherry sized)

1 cup all-purpose flour

2 eggs, beaten

2 cups panko flour

½ tsp kosher salt

1 tsp parsley, chopped (optional)

tomato sauce (optional)

DIRECTIONS

Drain mozzarella and pat dry with paper towels. Roll mozzarella balls in flour and shake off excess.

Combine panko with kosher salt.

Place mozzarella balls in egg mix and cover thoroughly, then place in panko mix to cover.

Place mozzarella balls, 6-8 per round, into Air Fryer in 1 layer. Air Fry for 8 minutes.

Let cool 1 minute before removing from Air Fryer. Garnish with fresh parsley. Serve with tomato sauce, if desired.

Temperature: 390ºF   Time: 5 minutes

FETA TRIANGLES

INGREDIENTS

1 egg yolk

4 ounces feta cheese

2 tbsp flat-leafed parsley, finely chopped

1 scallion, finely chopped

2 sheets of frozen filo pastry, defrosted

2 tablespoons olive oil

ground black pepper, to taste

DIRECTIONS

Beat the egg yolk in a bowl and mix in the feta, parsley, and scallion; season with pepper to taste.

Cut each sheet of filo dough into three strips. Scoop a full teaspoon of the feta mixture on the underside of a strip of pastry.

Fold one corner of the pastry over the filling to form a triangle, folding the strip in a zigzag manner until the filling is wrapped in a triangle.

Repeat until all the filo and feta has been used. Brush the filo with a little oil and place six triangles in the Air Fryer Basket. Slide the Basket into the Air Fryer and cook for 3 minutes at 390°F.

Turn the temperature down to 360°F and then cook for 2 minutes, or until golden brown. Serve the triangles.

Temperature: 400ºF   Time: 15 minutes

JAMÓN CROQUETTES

INGREDIENTS

1 cup mashed potatoes

¼ cup jamón (Spanish ham), chopped

kosher salt, to taste

ground black pepper, to taste

1 cup all-purpose flour

2 eggs, beaten

2 cups unsalted, plain breadcrumbs

DIRECTIONS

Mix together mashed potatoes and jamón with salt and black pepper until thoroughly combined. Scoop mashed potato mix and roll to create 1 ½ inch size balls, then press slightly to create a cylindrical shape.

Dredge croquettes in all-purpose flour and shake off excess. Dip croquettes in egg mix, then breadcrumbs to cover thoroughly.

Place 6 croquettes into the Air Fryer in one layer. Fry for 15 minutes. Remove and serve with aioli of your choice, if desired.

CURRY FRIED OKRA

INGREDIENTS

1 cup okra, sliced lengthwise into 4 pieces

¼ tsp kosher salt

½ to ¾ tsp curry powder (depending on your preference)

¼ tsp cornstarch

DIRECTIONS

Toss okra with kosher salt and curry powder. Add cornstarch and toss until thoroughly mixed.

Place in Air Fryer and fry 15 minutes at 400°F.

Temperature: 400ºF   Time: 20 minutes

EGG ROLLS

INGREDIENTS

1 lb ground pork

2 cups garlic chives, cut into 2-3" slices

1 cup shiitake mushroom, sliced

2 cups carrots, shredded

1 tbsp peanut oil

2 tsp Thai shrimp paste

Thai soy sauce, to taste

10-15 egg roll wrappers

vegetable oil, as needed

DIRECTIONS

Heat peanut oil in a large sauté pan on medium. Add pork and cook 3-5 minutes, breaking up large chunks. Add garlic chives, shiitake mushroom, carrots, shrimp paste and soy sauce. Cook 10-15 minutes, stirring, until pork is mostly cooked through moisture from vegetables has evaporated from the pan. Remove from heat and let cool.

Place approximately 3 tbsp of mixture at the base of egg roll wrapper, ½ inch from the bottom edge and ½ inch from the sides. Tuck in both sides and roll the wrapper to enclose mixture. Wet the top ½ inch of the egg roll wrapper to seal roll.

Place 2-3 egg rolls in Air Fryer in one layer, avoiding overlapping or wrappers touching each other. Drizzle with vegetable oil. Fry 10 minutes until wrappers are golden brown on top. Flip egg rolls and fry another 10 minutes.

Temperature: 400ºF   Time: 25–27 minutes

MEXICAN STREET CORN

INGREDIENTS

4 ears of corn, husked & cleaned

¼ cup mayonnaise

½ tsp ancho chile powder

1 lime, juiced

Toppings

Cotija cheese, grated

limes, in wedges

cilantro, chopped

DIRECTIONS

Place corn, 2 at a time, into Air Fryer and fry for 20-25 minutes until cooked through or lightly charred at ends. Combine mayonnaise, ancho chile, and lime juice. Mix to incorporate.

Remove corn carefully and lather in mayonnaise mixture. Place corn back into Air Fryer and fry 2-3 minutes.

Using tongs, remove corn and top with Cotija cheese. Serve with lime wedges and cilantro.

Temperature: 400ºF   Time: 25–30 minutes

FIVE SPICE CHICKEN WINGS

INGREDIENTS

4 complete chicken wings, split into flats and drumsticks

½ tsp kosher salt

1 tsp Chinese 5 spice powder

½ cup all-purpose flour

1 tsp vegetable oil

DIRECTIONS

Place chicken wings on paper towels and pat to dry thoroughly. Toss with kosher salt and Chinese 5 spice powder.

Dredge chicken wings in all-purpose flour and shake off excess. Toss chicken wings with vegetable oil.

Place only flats or only drumsticks in the Air Fryer and fry 25 minutes for flats and 30 minutes for drumsticks.

Temperature: 350ºF   Time: 20 minutes

GRILLED CHEESE

INGREDIENTS

2 slices white, whole wheat, or potato bread

½ cup to ⅔ cup sharp cheddar, shredded

1 tbsp butter, melted

DIRECTIONS

Spread shredded cheddar evenly between sliced bread.

Place sandwich into Air Fryer and fry for 10 minutes.

Remove from Air Fryer and brush both sides with melted butter. Serve with tomato soup, if desired.

ARANCINI

INGREDIENTS

Risotto Rice

2 tsp vegetable oil

1 cup arborio rice

2 tbsp shallots, minced

2 tsp garlic, minced

2 tbsp mushrooms, minced (optional)

1 tbsp dry white wine (optional)

3 cups unsalted chicken or vegetable stock

kosher salt, to taste

ground black pepper, to taste

Arancini

2 cups all-purpose flour

4 eggs, beaten

2 cups unsalted, unseasoned breadcrumbs

Toppings

lemon, wedges (optional)

parmesan cheese, grated (optional)

parsley, chopped (optional)

DIRECTIONS

Heat vegetable oil in a medium-sized sauté pan over medium heat until loose enough to coat the bottom of the pan. Add arborio rice and toast, 2-3 minutes. Reduce heat to medium-low. Add shallots, garlic, mushroom and sauté 2-3 minutes. Add white wine and cook 1-2 minutes until wine has been absorbed by rice. Heat chicken stock in a small pot until warm, but not hot. Begin to add chicken stock to sauté pan, ½ cup at a time, while stirring continuously. Do not add additional chicken stock until all the stock from the prior addition has been absorbed by the rice. Continue until rice is al dente to your liking. Season to taste with salt and pepper. Spread risotto on clean sheet tray and refrigerate until cool.

Roll risotto into 1½ inch bite-sized balls. Dredge in all-purpose flour and shake off excess.

Dip risotto balls into egg mix, then breadcrumbs to cover thoroughly. Place 6 arancini balls into the Air Fryer in one layer. Fry for 15 minutes. Remove and top arancini with parsley and parmesan cheese, if desired, and serve with lemon wedges.

OYSTERS ROCKEFELLER

INGREDIENTS

2 tbsp unsalted butter

3 cloves garlic, sliced

1 tbsp chives, chopped

1 tbsp tarragon, leaves only, chopped

5 oz spinach, chopped

2 tsp Pernod

¼ cup unsalted, plain breadcrumbs

¼ cup parmesan, grated

½ lemon, juiced

kosher salt

ground black pepper

DIRECTIONS

Melt butter in a medium sauté pan on low-medium heat. Add garlic, chives, tarragon and spinach. Cook 4-5 minutes until all greens are wilted and majority of the water has evaporated. Deglaze pan with Pernod and cook 1 minute until it has evaporated.

Remove mixture from heat and transfer to food processor or blender. Add breadcrumbs, parmesan, and lemon juice. Pulse until mixture is combined.

Season with kosher salt and ground black pepper to taste.

Place 4-6 oysters in Air Fryer, in one layer, and top with 2 tsp - 1 tbsp of spinach mixture, depending on oyster size. Fry for 8-10 minutes until oysters are cooked and topping is hot and bubbly.

Temperature: 400ºF Time: 10 minutes

PANZANELLA SALAD

INGREDIENTS

Toasted Bread

½ French baguette, sliced into 1" slices, cubed

1 tsp extra virgin olive oil

¼ tsp kosher salt

Basil Dressing

1 tsp shallot or red onion, minced

2 tbsp basil, chopped

1 clove garlic

¼ cup tomato, chopped

½ lemon, juiced

¼ cup extra virgin olive oil

kosher salt, to taste

ground black pepper, to taste

Salad

2 heirloom tomatoes, chopped

2 tsp shallot or red onion, minced

1 tbsp basil, chiffonade

ground black pepper, to taste

DIRECTIONS

Place baguette cubes in Air Fryer and toss with olive oil and salt. Fry for 10 minutes. In small blender, combine all ingredients for Basil Dressing and purée until smooth.

Season with salt and pepper to taste. For salad, combine toasted bread with tomatoes, shallot and Basil Dressing.

Toss well and let sit, 2-3 minutes, to allow dressing to permeate the bread. Garnish with basil and ground black pepper.

Temperature: 400ºF   Time: 25–30 minutes

SRIRACHA CHICKEN WINGS

INGREDIENTS

4 complete chicken wings, split into flats and drumsticks

½ cup sriracha

½ cup all-purpose flour

1 cup unsalted, plain breadcrumbs

DIRECTIONS

Place chicken wings on paper towels and pat to dry thoroughly. Dredge chicken wings in all-purpose flour and shake off excess.

Dip chicken wings in Sriracha, then breadcrumbs to cover thoroughly.

Place only flats or only drumsticks in Air Fryer and fry 25 minutes for flats and 30 minutes for drumsticks.

TUSCAN FLATBREAD PIZZA

INGREDIENTS

6 oz pizza dough

1 cup arugula leaves

1 cup sliced crimini mushrooms

2 tbsp rosemary, chopped

2 tbsp flat leaf parsley, chopped

2 garlic cloves, minced

½ cup Parmigiano-Reggiano cheese, shaved

4 oz mozzarella cheese, shredded

2 tbsp extra virgin olive oil

kosher salt

Black pepper, freshly ground

1 tbsp flour for dusting

Olive oil for brushing

DIRECTIONS

This recipe makes 2 pizzas. Lightly brush the basket of the Air Fryer with olive oil. If using a pizza pan, brush the inside of the pan with olive oil for easy release. Dust your work surface with flour. Separate your dough into two pieces. Flatten the first pizza dough before transferring into the bottom of the pan or basket.

Mix the olive oil, chopped rosemary, parsley, minced garlic and salt in a small mixing bowl. Using a pastry brush, coat the top of the dough. Cover the dough with 2 oz (½ cup) of the shredded mozzarella cheese. Layer with half the sliced mushrooms and arugula, then drizzle with the remaining oil. Finish the top with ¼ cup of the shaved Parmigiano.

Bake in the Air Fryer at 325°F for 10-12 minutes, checking periodically to make sure the pizza is not burning. Repeat steps with the second pizza.

PRO TIP

You can assemble these pizzas ahead of time and freeze them if you parbake the dough in advance. To prebake the dough, place the flattened dough in the Air Fryer or in the oven at 400°F for 2-3 minutes and then remove, let cool and top with your toppings before freezing.

Temperature: 400ºF   Time: 15 minutes

SCOTCH EGGS

INGREDIENTS

4 eggs, hard boiled

1 lb ground beef

¼ tsp dried parsley

¼ tsp dried thyme

¼ tsp garlic powder

¼ tsp onion powder

2 tsp kosher salt

¼ tsp ground black pepper

⅛ tsp cayenne pepper (optional)

1 tsp Dijon mustard

1 cup all-purpose flour

2 eggs, beaten

2 cups unsalted, plain breadcrumbs

DIRECTIONS

Combine ground beef with parsley, thyme, garlic powder, onion powder, salt, black pepper, cayenne pepper and mustard. Mix thoroughly. Dredge hardboiled egg in all-purpose flour and shake off excess. Form oval patty with ground beef mixture and place hardboiled egg at center. Gently mold ground beef around hardboiled egg to cover it completely.

Dredge scotch egg in all-purpose flour and shake off excess. Dip scotch egg in egg mix, then breadcrumbs to cover.

Place in Air Fryer, two at a time, and fry at 400ºF for 15 minutes until ground beef is completely cooked. Slice in half and serve with fresh parsley and chives, if desired.

Temperature: 400ºF Time: 10 minutes

SHRIMP & CHIVE POTSTICKERS

INGREDIENTS

1 tsp sesame oil

½ cup garlic chive, sliced thinly

½ cup shiitake mushroom, minced (optional)

1 cup fresh shrimp, peeled, deveined, minced or puréed in food processor

1 tbsp soy sauce

10-15 square wonton wrappers, cut into large circles

1 tbsp vegetable oil

cold water

DIRECTIONS

Heat sesame oil in medium sauté pan over medium heat. Add garlic chive, shiitake mushroom and 1 tsp soy sauce and cook 1-2 minutes. Add shrimp and soy sauce and cook another minute. Remove from heat. Place 2 tsp of shrimp mixture at center of circular wonton wrapper. Carefully wet all inner edges of wonton wrapper with cold water. Fold wonton wrapper in half to form a half-moon and seal edges. Brush pot-stickers with vegetable oil.

Place potstickers, 4-5 per batch, into Air Fryer, careful they do not rest on top of each other. Fry at 400°F for 10 minutes, or until puffy.

PRO TIP

Use wonton wrappers instead of dumpling wrappers. Wonton wrappers are thinner skinned and will fry up more easily with better crunch!

Temperature: 350ºF   Time: 20 minutes

SPRING ROLLS

INGREDIENTS

1 cup garlic chives, cut into 2-3" slices

2 cups shiitake mushrooms, sliced

1 cup mung bean sprouts

2 cups red or green cabbage, shredded

2 tsp toasted sesame oil

1 tsp chili oil (optional)

soy sauce, to taste

10-15 spring roll wrappers

DIRECTIONS

Heat sesame and chili oil in large sauté pan on medium heat until slick and shiny. Add garlic chives, shiitake mushroom, bean sprouts, cabbage and soy sauce. Cook 10-15 minutes, stirring, until vegetables have cooked through and moisture has evaporated from the pan. Remove from heat and let cool until cool to the touch.

Place approximately 2 tbsp of mixture of in straight line at base of spring roll wrapper, ½ inch from bottom edge and ¼ inch from sides. Tuck in both sides and roll spring roll wrapper to enclose mixture. Wet the top ½ inch of spring roll wrapper to seal roll.

Place 3-4 rolls in Air Fryer in one layer, avoiding overlapping or wrappers touching each other. Fry 12-15 minutes until wrappers are golden brown.

Temperature: 350ºF   Time: 18–22 minutes

AIR FRYER SAMOSAS

INGREDIENTS

20 samosa wrappers

¼ lb boiled and peeled potatoes

30g green peas, cooked

½ tsp chilli powder

1 tbsp finely chopped coriander leaves

1 tsp oil

½ tsp cumin seeds

½ tsp turmeric powder

½ tsp garam masala

salt to taste

1 tsp of oil (for brushing)

DIRECTIONS

Thaw the samosa wrappers if they are frozen. Heat oil in a pan, add cumin seeds and allow them to crackle. Add boiled green peas, turmeric powder, salt, chilli powder and garam masala. Mix well. Add cubed or roughly chopped potatoes to the mixture and mix again. If needed, sprinkle 1 tsp of water. Sprinkle some coriander leaves, remove from the flame and set the mixture aside.

Carefully lay out the samosa wrappers. Place a small portion of the samosa mixture onto left corner of each wrapper. Seal the samosa by folding from the opposite edge and carefully turn them over until you achieve a cone shape. Wet the edges of the patty and give them a gently press.

Repeat the process for the rest of the samosas. Remember to cover the prepared samosas with a damp muslin cloth.

Preheat the Air Fryer for 5 minutes at 350°F. Brush the samosas with oil.

Arrange 5 samosas in the Air Fryer basket and cook for 18-22 minutes, or until golden brown. Repeat the process for the remaining samosas.

STUFFED BAKED POTATO

INGREDIENTS

Baked Potato

1 russet potato, halved

1 tsp olive oil

½ tsp kosher salt

Mashed Potato

2 tbsp whole milk

2 tsp chives, minced

1 dash garlic powder (optional)

1 tbsp cheddar cheese, grated (optional)

1 tbsp bacon, chopped, cooked (optional)

kosher salt

ground black pepper

Topping

1 tbsp Greek yogurt

2 tsp dill, chopped

DIRECTIONS

Drizzle potato with olive oil and salt. Place in Air Fryer and fry for 45 minutes. Remove potato from Air Fryer and let cool 5 minutes. Carefully scoop out inside of potato, leaving ½" of the inside intact to hold potato's shape.

Remove skin from potato innards and place in small bowl with milk, chives, garlic powder, cheddar cheese, bacon. Mash to combine. Season with kosher salt and ground black pepper to taste.

Place mashed potato back into Baked Potato and fry another 2-3 minutes, if desired. Remove potato from Air Fryer and top with Greek yogurt and dill.

PORK & SHIITAKE DUMPLINGS

INGREDIENTS

1 lb ground pork

3 tbsp soy sauce

½ cup garlic chive, sliced thinly

½ cup shiitake mushroom, minced

1 egg, beaten

½ tsp ginger, minced

¼ tsp ground white pepper

1 tsp sesame oil

25-30 wonton wrappers, cut into large circles

cold water

1 tbsp vegetable oil

DIRECTIONS

Combine ground pork, soy sauce, garlic chive, shiitake, egg, ginger, white pepper, sesame oil in large bowl and mix by hand thoroughly to combine. Place wonton wrapper on flat surface and add 2 tsp pork mixture to center.

Wet all edges of wonton wrapper and fold in half to form a half moon shape. If desired, overlap edges along the outer edge of wrapper to form a layered effect. Brush with vegetable oil. Place dumplings, 5 at a time, standing upright, to Air Fryer. Fry at 400ºF for 10 minutes.

PRO TIP

For more even browning, turn dumplings 180 degrees halfway through the frying process.

Temperature: 390ºF   Time: 10 minutes

CHICKEN & WAFFLE SLIDERS

INGREDIENTS

frozen mini waffles, toasted

frozen breaded chicken tenders

DIRECTIONS

Take 1 chicken tender and place it between two toasted mini waffles.

Secure the chicken tender with a skewer. Repeat until all the chicken tenders and frozen waffles are gone.

Air fry the sliders in batches at 390°F for 10 minutes, checking to make sure that they are crispy.

Cajun Fried Chicken Thighs, pg. 65

ENTRÉES

Temperature: 375ºF   Time: 10 minutes

AIR FRYER BURGER

INGREDIENTS

1 lb ground beef, 90% lean

1 egg, beaten

¼ cup panko breadcrumbs

½ tsp garlic powder

½ tsp onion powder

½ tsp smoked paprika

½ tsp ground black pepper

2 tsp kosher salt

½ tsp Worcestershire sauce

⅛ tsp cayenne pepper (optional)

DIRECTIONS

Combine all ingredients for the burgers in one large bowl and mix by hand until thoroughly combined.

Form into 4-5" patties and place, two patties at a time, into Air Fryer.

Air fry at 375°F for 10 minutes or until desired doneness. Serve with desired burger bun and accompaniments.

Temperature: 330ºF   Time: 45 minutes

GARDEN FRITTATA

INGREDIENTS

6 eggs

4 cups button mushrooms, cleaned

1 red onion

2 tbsp olive oil

6 tbsp feta cheese, crumbled

1 pinch salt

DIRECTIONS

Peel and slice a red onion into ¼ inch thin slices. Clean the button mushrooms; then cut into ¼ inch thin slices. In a sauté pan with olive oil, sweat the onions and mushrooms under a medium flame until tender. Remove from heat and place on a dry kitchen towel to cool.

Preheat the Air Fryer to 330°F. In a mixing bowl, crack 6 eggs and whisk thoroughly, adding a pinch of salt.

In an 8-in. heat-resistant baking dish, coat the inside and bottom with a light coating of pan spray. Pour the eggs into the baking dish, then the onion and mushroom mixture, and then the cheese.

Place the baking dish in the Air Fryer and cook for 27 to 30 minutes. The frittata is done when the knife comes out clean.

Temperature: 350ºF   Time: 20 minutes

LEMON PEPPER AIR FRYER CHICKEN

INGREDIENTS

2 chicken breasts

2 lemons, sliced

1 tsp garlic purée

1 tsp black peppercorns

salt & pepper

DIRECTIONS

Preheat the Air Fryer to 350°F. Lay your chicken breasts onto a chopping board. Season each side with salt and pepper, then add your lemon slices to the tops of each chicken breast. Wrap the chicken breasts in tin foil with the lemon slices and seasonings.

Place the tin foil-wrapped chicken breasts in the Air Fryer and cook at 350°F for 20 minutes. Check to see if they are fully cooked before serving, if not, cook for an additional few minutes.

Temperature: 200ºF   Time: 5 minutes

AIR FRYER RAVIOLIS

INGREDIENTS

1 jar marinara sauce, store-bought

1 box cheese ravioli, store-bought or meat ravioli

2 cups Italian-style bread crumbs

1 cup buttermilk

¼ cup Parmesan cheese

DIRECTIONS

Dip each ravioli in buttermilk. Add about a tablespoon of olive oil to the breadcrumbs, then roll each ravioli into the crumb mixture.

Place the breaded ravioli into your Air Fryer and cook for about 5 minutes, or until crispy.

Serve warm with marinara sauce for dipping.

BAJA FISH TACOS

INGREDIENTS

Crispy Fish

8oz fish of your choice, sliced into 2" pieces

½ tsp kosher salt

1 cup all-purpose flour

2 eggs, beaten

1 cup unsalted, plain breadcrumbs

Tacos

6-10 8" corn tortillas

2 tsp vegetable oil

¼ cup red onion, sliced thinly

1 red bell pepper, sliced thinly

1 avocado, sliced thinly

1 lime, wedges

1 tbsp cilantro, chopped

1 jalapeño, sliced thinly (optional)

2 tbsp sour cream (optional)

DIRECTIONS

Toss fish with salt. Dredge fish pieces in all-purpose flour and shake off excess. Dip fish into egg mixture, then breadcrumbs to cover thoroughly. Air fry at 400°F for 15-20 minutes until completely cooked through.

In a small sauté pan, heat vegetable oil on medium heat until slick and shiny. Add onion and red bell pepper with a pinch of kosher salt. Sauté 2-3 minutes until onion is translucent.

Preheat oven to 350°F. Place corn tortillas directly on an oven rack and let bake 5 minutes until hot.

Assemble tacos with fish, onion, red bell pepper, avocado and garnish with lime, cilantro, jalapeño and sour cream.

Temperature: 400ºF   Time: 10–15 minutes

CHICKEN FRIED STEAK

INGREDIENTS

1 lb sirloin beef

½ tsp kosher salt

¼ tsp garlic powder

¼ tsp onion powder

¼ tsp ground black pepper

1 cup all-purpose flour

1 cup buttermilk

1 tbsp hot sauce

1 cup unsalted, plain breadcrumbs

DIRECTIONS

Cut beef into 4 oz pieces and wrap them loosely in plastic wrap. Pound with a mallet until each piece is approximately ¼" thick. Season beef with salt, garlic powder, onion powder, and black pepper. Dredge the beef in all-purpose flour and shake off excess. Mix the buttermilk with hot sauce and whisk to combine. Dip each piece of beef in the buttermilk mix and let the excess drip off. Dredge the beef in breadcrumbs and shake off any excess. Place 1 piece of beef in the Air Fryer and air fry for 5-7 minutes. Flip beef over. Air fry for another 5-7 minutes.

PRO TIP

Total time of 10 minutes will result in a medium rare steak. For a more well-done steak, increase the time to 12-15 minutes total.

BUTTERMILK FRIED CHICKEN

INGREDIENTS

1 lb chicken thighs and drumsticks, bone in

2 tsp kosher salt

1 cup buttermilk

2 cups unsalted, plain breadcrumbs

1 tbsp unsalted Cajun seasoning

DIRECTIONS

Toss chicken with salt and place in medium bowl. Cover with buttermilk and mix to coat thoroughly. Let marinate in refrigerator 4 hours minimum. Combine breadcrumbs with Cajun seasoning and mix thoroughly.

Remove chicken from buttermilk and shake gently to drain excess. Dredge chicken in breadcrumbs until fully covered.

Place in the Air Fryer, 2-3 pieces at a time, in one layer. Air fry at 400°F for 25 minutes until the chicken is fully cooked and juices run clear.

Temperature: 400ºF   Time: 20-25 minutes

CAJUN FRIED CHICKEN THIGHS

INGREDIENTS

6 chicken thighs, boneless, skinless

2 tsp kosher salt

1 tbsp unsalted Cajun seasoning

1 cup all-purpose flour

2 eggs, beaten

2 cups unsalted, plain breadcrumbs

DIRECTIONS

Toss chicken thighs with salt and Cajun seasoning until well covered. Dredge thighs into flour and shake off excess. Dip thighs in egg mix, then breadcrumbs to cover thoroughly.

Place thighs 2 at a time into the Air Fryer and air fry for 20-25 minutes, or until the internal temperature of the thighs reaches 178°F, and juices run clear. Serve with maple syrup, if desired.

CARNE ASADA TACOS

INGREDIENTS

Marinated Flank Steak

1lb flank steak, cut into minimum number of pieces fitting Air Fryer (usually 2)

1 cup orange juice

4 cloves garlic, minced

2 shallots, minced

1 cup cilantro, chopped

2 habanero peppers, seeded, chopped (optional)

3 tbsp soy sauce

4 adobo peppers in chipotle sauce, chopped

1 lime, juiced

15 grinds black pepper

¼ cup basil, chopped

1 tbsp vegetable oil

For Tacos

8" corn tortillas

¼ cup cilantro, chopped

½ avocado, sliced

10 cherry tomatoes, halved

DIRECTIONS

Combine flank steak with marinade ingredients and toss to mix thoroughly. Let marinate for a minimum of 4 hours, or overnight. Remove steak from marinade. Heat a medium sauté pan with the vegetable oil on high heat. Add the steak and sear each side for 2-3 minutes, or until well browned. Place the steak into the Air Fryer, 1 at a time, and air fry for 30-40 minutes depending on desired doneness. Pour the remainder of marinade into a sauté pan and cook on medium heat for 10-15 minutes. Remove the marinade from the heat and strain to extract jus. Remove steak from the Air Fryer and let rest for 10 minutes. Slice into ½" cubes. Assemble tacos with corn tortillas, steak, avocado, tomato, and cilantro. Serve with small bowl of jus, if desired.

PRO TIPS

30 minutes will result in a medium-rare steak. Add time for more well-done steaks.

Cooking the marinade for longer periods of time will result in thicker and saltier just as the water reduces. Adjust cooking times depending on your level of desired thickness and taste.

Temperature: 350ºF   Time: 20–25 minutes

FALAFEL

INGREDIENTS

1 can chickpeas, drained, rinsed, spun dry

2 cloves garlic

½ cup red onion, chopped

2 tbsp dill, chopped

2 tbsp parsley, chopped

2 tbsp - ¼ cup all-purpose flour

1 tsp kosher salt

¼ tsp ground cumin

¼ tsp paprika

1 dash cayenne pepper (optional)

1 dash cinnamon (optional)

¼ tsp white sugar

10 grinds black pepper

1 tbsp olive oil

DIRECTIONS

Combine chickpeas, garlic, onion, dill, parsley, salt, cumin, paprika, cayenne, cinnamon, black pepper in food processor and pulse until smooth. Add all-purpose flour, 1 tbsp at a time, until mixture is moist but not wet and can be easily formed into balls.

Wet hands with olive oil. Scoop 1 tbsp of falafel mix at a time and form into round balls.

Place 5-6 falafel into the Air Fryer, in one layer, and air fry for 10 minutes. Flip the falafel balls. Air fry for another 10-25 minutes, or until falafel balls are brown on the inside and cooked entirely.

Temperature: 400ºF   Time: 15 minutes

FRIED PORK CUTLET

INGREDIENTS

½ lb pork tenderloin, cut into 2" - 2.5" pieces

1 tsp kosher salt

1 cup all-purpose flour

2 eggs, beaten

2 cups unsalted, plain breadcrumbs

DIRECTIONS

Wrap each piece of pork tenderloin loosely in plastic wrap. Pound with a mallet until each piece is approximately ½" thick. Toss all pork cutlets with kosher salt.

Dredge pork cutlets in all-purpose flour and shake off any excess. Dip pork cutlets in egg mixture, then breadcrumbs to cover thoroughly.

Place in the Air Fryer, 1-2 at a time, in one single layer and air fry at 400ºF for 15 minutes.

FISH
& CHIPS

INGREDIENTS

Fish

½ lb (8 oz) mild, flaky white fish fillets, skin off and cut into 2-3 oz pieces

1 tsp kosher salt

¼ tsp ground black pepper

½ cup all-purpose flour

2 eggs, beaten

1 cup panko flour

1 tsp parsley, chopped

Chips

2 cups golden yukon or russet potatoes, diced

1 tsp vegetable oil

½ tsp kosher salt

DIRECTIONS

Pat fish fillets dry with paper towels and season both sides with salt and ground black pepper. Dredge fish in all-purpose flour and shake off any excess. Dip fish in the egg mix, and then in the panko flour to coat thoroughly.

Place the pieces in the Air Fryer in one single layer. Air fry at 400°F for 25 minutes, or until the fish is fully cooked through. Remove fish from the Air Fryer and top with parsley. For potatoes, toss the potatoes with oil and salt. Place in the Air Fryer and fry at 400°F for 30 minutes.

Serve fish and potatoes together with tartar sauce and malt vinegar, if desired.

Temperature: 400ºF   Time: 12–15 minutes

CUMIN CRUSTED LAMB CHOPS

INGREDIENTS

4 lamb chops

1 tsp kosher salt

¼ tsp ground black pepper

1 tbsp whole cumin seed

1 tbsp whole fennel seed

Mint Yogurt

½ cup Greek yogurt

½ lemon, juiced

¼ cup mint, chopped

1 tbsp dill, chopped

1 scallion, chopped

kosher salt, to taste

DIRECTIONS

Toss lamb chops with salt and pepper. Using a spice grinder, pulse cumin seeds and fennel seeds 2-3 times until lightly coarse, but not pulverized. Rub the lamb chops with cumin and fennel mix to cover thoroughly.

Place lamb chops into the Air Fryer, with the frenched bone standing upright and overlapping as little as possible. Air fry for 12-15 minutes at 400°F, or to your desired doneness.

For mint yogurt; combine yogurt, lemon juice, mint, dill, and scallion in a blender and purée until smooth. Season with salt. Serve with lamb chops.

PRO TIP

12 minutes in the Air Fryer results in medium-rare lamb chops. Add additional time for more well-done chops.

ROAST PORK TENDERLOIN
WITH SAGE & CHERRY GLAZE

INGREDIENTS

Roast Pork Tenderloin

1 lb pork tenderloin

2 tsp kosher salt

1 tsp black pepper

2 tsp vegetable oil

¼ cup sage, minced

1 tbsp thyme, leaves only

Cherry Glaze

1 tsp shallot, minced

½ cup cherries, pitted, chopped

DIRECTIONS

Season pork tenderloin with kosher salt and black pepper. In a medium sauté pan, heat the vegetable oil. Sear the top side of the pork tenderloin in hot oil for 1-2 minutes until a brown crust forms. Place the pork tenderloin in the Air Fryer and cover with sage and thyme. Air fry for 20-25 minutes at 400°F or until desired doneness. Remove pork tenderloin from Air Fryer and let rest 5 minutes before slicing. Reduce the heat of your sauté pan to low. Add minced shallot and cherries. Cook for 3-5 minutes until shallots are translucent and cherries are soft. Transfer mixture to a blender and blend until smooth.

PRO TIP

20 minutes will result in a medium-rare pork tenderloin. Add more time as necessary for a more well done tenderloin.

Temperature: 350ºF   Time: 20 minutes

SESAME 'CHICKEN' STYLE TOFU

INGREDIENTS

1 block extra-firm tofu, drained, pressed, sliced in ½" thick rectangles

1 tsp vegetable oil

Sesame 'Chicken' Sauce

½ cup unsalted chicken stock

¼ cup soy sauce

3 tbsp white sugar

2 tbsp mirin

¼ tsp garlic, minced

¼ tsp ginger, peeled, minced

2 tsp sesame oil

1 tbsp sambal chili paste (optional)

1 tbsp cornstarch

¼ cup water

Toppings

1 tsp toasted white sesame seeds

1 scallion, sliced

DIRECTIONS

Toss tofu with vegetable oil. Separate tofu into 3-4 batches and place into the Air Fryer one batch at a time, in one even layer. Air fry for 20 minutes at 350°F, turning once halfway.

In a small sauté pan; combine the chicken stock, soy sauce, white sugar, mirin, garlic, ginger, sesame oil, and sambal over low heat. Whisk together cornstarch with water.

Once stock mixture is simmering, add the cornstarch slurry and whisk to combine, for about 1-2 minutes. Remove from heat and toss the tofu in the sesame sauce. Top with white sesame seeds and scallion.

Temperature: 400ºF   Time: 10 minutes

BLACKENED SALMON

INGREDIENTS

8 oz salmon fillet, skin on or off

½ tsp kosher salt

1 tsp unsalted blackening seasoning

2 tsp parsley, chopped (optional)

½ lemon, wedges (optional)

DIRECTIONS

Season the salmon on both sides with salt and blackening seasoning. Air fry the salmon at 400°F for 10-15 minutes, depending on desired level of doneness. Serve with lemon and parsley, if desired.

PRO TIP

You can place your skin-on fillet on aluminum foil to avoid sticking to the Air Fryer if you do not have nonstick spray.

10 minutes results in medium-rare salmon. Add additional time for well-done salmon.

Temperature: 390ºF Time: 8 minutes

AIR FRYER SHRIMP SCAMPI

INGREDIENTS

7 medium shrimp, peeled and deveined

1 tbsp chopped parsley for garnish

Marinade

1 tbsp olive oil

1 garlic clove, minced

½ tbsp butter, melted

¼ cup white wine

½ lemon, juiced

DIRECTIONS

Mix together the olive oil, minced garlic, butter, white wine, and lemon juice. Add the shrimp and toss to coat.

Preheat your Air Fryer to 390°F and add your marinated shrimp. Air fry for up to 8 minutes, checking to ensure that the shrimp are done correctly.

Serve and garnish with chopped parsley.

SNACKS

AVOCADO FRIES

INGREDIENTS

1 avocado, pitted and sliced

¼ cup all-purpose flour

1 egg, beaten

½ cup panko breadcrumbs

¼ tsp kosher salt

DIRECTIONS

Carefully scoop avocado slices from avocado and separate. Place all-purpose flour in one large bowl, beaten egg in one large bowl, and panko breadcrumbs with salt in final large bowl.

Dredge avocado in all-purpose flour and shake to remove excess flour. Coat avocado in egg mixture, then panko breadcrumbs. Shake avocado to remove excess panko breadcrumbs.

Place into Air Fryer. Fry at 400ºF for 10 minutes, shaking once halfway through cycle.

Temperature: 400°F   Time: 15 minutes

CAULIFLOWER BUFFALO BITES

INGREDIENTS

Buffalo Sauce

1 tbsp unsalted butter

⅓ cup hot sauce

1 tsp honey

1 dash garlic powder

Cauliflower

4 cups cauliflower florets, sliced into ¼ inch pieces

1 tbsp vegetable oil

DIRECTIONS

Toss cauliflower with oil. Place cauliflower florets into Air Fryer in 2 batches. Fry at 400°F for 15 minutes, shaking once or twice throughout the cycle.

Melt butter in a small saucepan over medium-low heat. Add hot sauce, honey, and garlic powder to the butter and whisk to combine.

Toss the cauliflower florets with the hot sauce mixture and drain any extra sauce. Serve immediately.

Temperature: 400°F   Time: 20 minutes

ZUCCHINI WEDGES

INGREDIENTS

3 cups zucchini, sliced into
¼" thick rectangular fries
(approx. 1 zucchini)

1 cup all-purpose flour

3 large eggs, beaten

2 cups panko breadcrumbs

1 tsp kosher salt

1 tsp parmesan cheese, grated
(optional)

DIRECTIONS

Toss zucchini with flour and shake off excess. Dip zucchini wedges into the egg to coat, then toss thoroughly into the panko.

Place 1 cup of wedges at a time into Air Fryer and air fry for 20 minutes at 400°F, shaking once halfway through cooking.

Temperature: 400ºF   Time: 10 minutes

CRUNCHY DILL PICKLES

INGREDIENTS

Special Dip

2 tbsp mayonnaise

2 tbsp ketchup

¼ tsp yellow onion, minced

Pickles

1 cup dill pickles, sliced into ¼ inch thick circles

½ cup all-purpose flour

2 large eggs, beaten

1 cup panko breadcrumbs

1 tsp Cajun seasoning

1 tsp dried basil

1 tsp dried oregano

DIRECTIONS

Placed the sliced pickles on paper towels and pat dry. Place all-purpose flour in one large bowl, beaten eggs in another large bowl, and panko breadcrumbs with Cajun seasoning and herbs in a final large bowl.

Dredge the pickles with all-purpose flour and shake to remove the excess. Coat the pickles in the egg mixture, then in the panko breadcrumbs.

Shake pickles to remove any excess. Place them into the Air Fryer. Fry at 400°F for 10 minutes or until crispy, shaking once halfway through the cycle.

Mix the mayonnaise, ketchup, and minced onion together to serve as a dip, if desired.

CRISPY KALE CHIPS

INGREDIENTS

1 bunch dinosaur kale, stemmed, chopped into large pieces

½ tsp kosher salt

2 tsp olive oil

Mexican Inspired

¼ tsp ancho chile powder

1 tsp lime juice

Indian Inspired

¼ tsp curry powder

¼ tsp garam masala

Chinese Inspired

Substitute sesame oil for olive oil

1 tsp soy sauce

Spanish Inspired

¼ tsp smoked paprika

¼ tsp pimento pepper flakes

⅛ tsp garlic powder

DIRECTIONS

Toss kale with salt, olive oil and your choice of toppings. Place into Air Fryer, roughly 1 cup at a time. Air fry for 5 minutes before checking. Shake and air fry for another 1-3 minutes, depending on how crispy you like your chips.

Temperature: 400ºF   Time: 30 minutes

SEASONED AIR FRYER CHICKPEAS

INGREDIENTS

1 (15 oz) can chickpeas, drained, rinsed and patted dry

1 tsp vegetable oil

½ tsp kosher salt

¼ tsp garlic powder

¼ tsp paprika

¼ tsp ancho chile

2 tsp fresh lemon juice

DIRECTIONS

Toss the chickpeas with oil and salt. Transfer to the Air Fryer and air fry at 400°F for 20 minutes.

Add garlic powder, paprika, ancho chile, and lemon juice and toss to combine. Air fry for another 10 minutes.

TORTILLA CHIPS

INGREDIENTS

4 8" corn tortillas, cut into eighths

⅛ tsp kosher salt

DIRECTIONS

Divide tortilla triangles into 2 batches. Place 1 batch in Air Fryer and air fry at 400°F for 15 minutes, shaking once roughly halfway through cooking.

Remove and top with half of the salt. Repeat with second batch.

Temperature: 400°F   Time: 10 minutes

POTATO CHIPS

INGREDIENTS

1 russet potato, thinly sliced with a mandoline

½ tsp vegetable oil

¼ tsp kosher salt

DIRECTIONS

Place potato slices in cold water for 30 minutes. Rinse and pat dry with paper towels.

Toss potato slices with oil and kosher salt. Place potato chips in Air Fryer, one layer at a time, being careful to minimize overlap. Air fry for 10 minutes, shaking once halfway through cooking.

Southern Fried Okra, pg. 108

SIDES

Temperature: 400ºF   Time: 10 minutes

BRUSSELS SPROUTS
WITH SWEET THAI CHILE

INGREDIENTS

2 cups brussels sprouts, stemmed, halved, shaved thinly with knife

1 tsp vegetable oil

¼ tsp kosher salt

½ lemon, cut into wedges (optional)

Sweet Thai Chile

1 tbsp sambal

1 tsp rice vinegar

¼ cup water

1 tbsp white sugar

DIRECTIONS

Toss brussels sprouts with vegetable oil and salt. Place into Air Fryer and fry 10 minutes.

Heat water in small pot over low heat and add sugar. Stir until sugar is melted.

Remove from heat and add sambal and rice vinegar. Whisk to combine.

Serve brussels sprouts with lemon wedges and chile sauce.

Temperature: 400ºF   Time: 10–12 minutes

LEMONY GREEN BEANS

INGREDIENTS

1 lb green beans, washed and destemmed

1 lemon

¼ tsp oil

pinch of salt

black pepper to taste

DIRECTIONS

Put the green beans in the Air Fryer and add a few squeezes of lemon. Add the salt and pepper.

Drizzle oil over the top. Cook at 400°F degrees for 10-12 minutes.

AIR FRYER VEGETABLES

INGREDIENTS

2 cups baby carrots or carrot sticks

1 tsp vegetable oil

½ tsp kosher salt

⅛ tsp ground black pepper

1 tsp thyme, leaves only (optional)

Zucchini

1 cup green zucchini, cut into half-moons

1 cup yellow squash, cut into half-moons

½ tsp kosher salt

⅛ tsp ground white pepper (optional)

DIRECTIONS

Toss carrots with vegetable oil, salt, and black pepper. Place in Air Fryer and fry at 400ºF for 20 minutes, shaking once halfway through.

Add thyme and toss to mix thoroughly. Toss zucchini with salt and white pepper. Place in the Air Fryer, 1 cup at a time, and fry at 400ºF for 15 minutes.

Temperature: 400°F   Time: 12–15 minutes

CRISPY ROASTED BROCCOLI

INGREDIENTS

2 cups broccoli florets

2 tsp vegetable oil

½ tsp kosher salt

½ tsp garam masala powder

⅛ tsp chili powder

½ lemon, cut into wedges (optional)

DIRECTIONS

Toss broccoli florets with vegetable oil and salt. Place broccoli in Air Fryer and fry 12-15 minutes until desired level of crispiness.

Remove from Air Fryer and toss with garam masala powder and chili powder.

Serve with lemon wedges, if desired.

Temperature: 350ºF and 400ºF   Time: 15 minutes and 15 minutes

FRIED PLANTAINS

INGREDIENTS

2 cups plantains, peeled, sliced ¼" thick (approximately 2 plantains)

2 tsp vegetable oil (or 4 sprays of nonstick spray)

¼ tsp kosher salt

DIRECTIONS

Toss plantain slices in a large bowl with oil and salt. Place 1 cup in Air Fryer, moving pieces apart that are sticking together. Air fry for 15 minutes, remove and shake. Then fry at 400ºF for 15 minutes until well-browned. Remove all plantains and repeat with second cup. Serve with salsa verde and hot sauce, if desired.

PRO TIP

Choose plantains that are almost all black - these are perfectly ripe and will cook up to be wonderfully crunchy!

HASSELBACK POTATO

INGREDIENTS

1 russet potato

1 tsp kosher salt

1 tsp olive oil

1 tsp chives, minced

DIRECTIONS

Place potato on its side lengthwise. Pierce russet potato with a metal skewer along its entire length to serve as the stop guard for slicing.

Carefully slice potato into tiny thin slices without piercing through the bottom of the potato. Remove metal skewer.

Sprinkle potato with kosher salt and olive oil. Place potato in Air Fryer and fry 50-60 minutes until cooked through and tops are crispy.

Garnish with chives.

Temperature: 400ºF   Time: 15 minutes

SOUTHERN FRIED OKRA

INGREDIENTS

1 cup okra, sliced into ½" rounds

1 cup all-purpose flour

1 egg, beaten

1 cup panko flour

¼ tsp kosher salt

¼ tsp Cajun seasoning

DIRECTIONS

Toss okra in flour and shake off excess. Mix panko with salt and Cajun seasoning.

Place okra into egg mixture to coat, then panko mix to cover thoroughly. Place okra into Air Fryer and fry 15 minutes.

Temperature: 400°F   Time: 15 minutes

HUSH PUPPIES

INGREDIENTS

¾ cup cornmeal

½ cup all-purpose flour

1 tsp kosher salt

½ tsp baking powder

2 tsp Cajun seasoning

¼ cup unsalted butter

½ cup buttermilk

1 cup all-purpose flour

2 eggs, beaten

2 cups panko flour

DIRECTIONS

Melt butter and buttermilk in a small pot over low-medium heat until fully melted. Combine cornmeal, flour, salt, baking powder and Cajun seasoning in bowl. Whisk to combine.

Stir in flour mixture into butter mixture over low heat, mixing constantly as it forms a dough. Remove from heat.

Shape dough into 2" balls and dredge in all-purpose flour. Dip balls into egg mixture, then panko flour to cover thoroughly. Place 5-6 balls into Air Fryer in one single layer.

Fry at 400°F for 15 minutes, shaking once halfway through cooking.

Temperature: 400ºF Time: 15 minutes

ONION RINGS

INGREDIENTS

1 vidalia onion, peeled, ends cut off, sliced into ¾" rings

1 cup all-purpose flour

1 egg, beaten

1 cup panko breadcrumbs

½ tsp kosher salt

DIRECTIONS

Dredge onion rings in flour and shake off excess. Combine panko and salt. Dip onion rings in egg, then panko mixture to cover thoroughly.

Place into Air Fryer 4-6 at a time, overlapping rings as little as possible. Fry for 15 minutes.

Serve with ketchup and mustard, if desired.

Temperature: 400°F   Time: 15 minutes

POTATO LATKES

INGREDIENTS

2 cups russet potato, shredded

1 egg, beaten

3 tbsp - ¼ cup all-purpose flour

1 tsp kosher salt

¼ tsp garlic powder (optional)

¼ tsp onion powder (optional)

black pepper (optional)

DIRECTIONS

Soak shredded potatoes in cold water for 30 minutes. Rinse and pat dry on paper towels. Combine potato, egg, flour, salt, garlic powder, onion powder and black pepper in bowl and mix thoroughly.

Start with 3 tablespoons of flour and add another tablespoon if needed. Shape into flat 3" discs and place 3 at a time, in one layer, in Air Fryer.

Fry 10 minutes and flip latkes. Fry another 5 minutes. Serve with sour cream and chives or applesauce, if desired.

Temperature: 400ºF   Time: 5 minutes

EASY CRISPY BACON

INGREDIENTS

4 strips uncured bacon
(not thick-cut)

DIRECTIONS

Place 4 strips of bacon in Air Fryer, letting the sides of the bacon slide up the walls and ensuring bacon does not overlap. Fry at 370°F for 10 minutes. Remove and use paper towels to remove some of the grease on top of the bacon. Place back into Air Fry and fry at 400°F for 5 minutes. Drain on paper towels and serve.

PRO TIP

You can adjust the length of the last few minutes at 400°F depending on how crispy you like your bacon!

Temperature: 400ºF   Time: 25 minutes

LEMON SHISHITO PEPPERS

INGREDIENTS

10-12 shishito peppers

2 tsp vegetable oil

1 tsp kosher salt

½ lemon, cut into wedges (optional)

DIRECTIONS

Place shishitos into Air Fryer and toss with salt and vegetable oil.

Fry for 15 minutes. Squeeze fresh lemon onto shishitos and shake. Serve immediately.

Temperature: 350ºF and 400ºF Time: 10 minutes and 5 minutes

SWEET POTATO FRIES

INGREDIENTS

2 sweet potatoes, cut into ¼″ rectangular strips

¼ tsp cornstarch

¼ tsp kosher salt

DIRECTIONS

Place sweet potato strips into cold water. Let soak 30 minutes. Pat dry with paper towels. Toss sweet potatoes with cornstarch until just lightly coated.

Place one single layer of fries into Air Fryer and fry at 350ºF for 10 minutes.

Remove from Air Fryer and shake. Air fry again at 400ºF for 5 minutes. Toss immediately with salt.

Temperature: 320ºF–350ºF   Time: 30 minutes

AIR FRYER CHEESE & BACON MUFFINS

INGREDIENTS

1½ cups all-purpose flour

1 egg

4 slices bacon

1 onion, diced

3½ oz cheddar cheese

2 tsp baking powder

2 tbsp olive oil

1 cup whole milk

1 tsp chopped parsley

salt & pepper

DIRECTIONS

Sauté the bacon in a pan with a little olive oil. When the bacon is almost done, add the onion and then set to one side. Mix the parsley, baking powder, flour, grated cheese and mix together.

Add the milk, olive oil, and egg with a wooden spoon and then mix until it becomes a sticky, thick dough. Drain the oil from the bacon and onion and add to the mixture.

Add the mixture to six medium sized muffin tins and place them in the Air Fryer for 20 minutes on 350ºF, followed by a further 10 minutes on 320ºF to make sure they are cooked in the center.

PUMPKIN AND PORK EMPANADAS

INGREDIENTS

2 tbsp olive oil

1 lb ground pork

½ onion, diced

1½ cups pumpkin purée

3 tbsp water

1 red chili pepper, minced

½ tsp cinnamon

½ tsp dried thyme

1 tsp salt

freshly ground black pepper

1 package of 10 empanada discs, thawed

olive oil

DIRECTIONS

Pre-heat a medium sauté pan over medium-high heat. Add the pork and onions and sauté for about 5 minutes, or until the pork is browned and the onions are soft. Drain the fat from the pan and discard.

Add the pumpkin purée, water, red chili pepper, cinnamon, thyme, salt and pepper to the pork mixture in the pan. Stir to combine everything and simmer for 10 minutes. Remove the pan from the heat and set aside to cool.

Place the empanada discs on a flat surface and brush the edges with water. Place 2 to 3 tablespoons of the filling in the center of each disc. Fold the dough over the filling to form a half moon. Crimp the edges shut with the tip of a fork and brush both sides of the empanadas with olive oil. Depending on the size of your Air Fryer, place 3 to 5 empanadas into the Air Fryer. Air fry for 15 minutes, turning over after 8 minutes. Serve warm.

Cheesecake, pg. 129

DESSERTS

Temperature: 350ºF   Time: 3–5 minutes

EASY DONUTS

INGREDIENTS

1 can biscuit dough

3 tbsp melted butter

⅓ cup granulated sugar

½ tsp cinnamon (adjust to your taste)

4 tbsp dark brown sugar

pinch of allspice

DIRECTIONS

Combine the sugar, cinnamon, brown sugar, and allspice in a small bowl and set aside. Remove biscuits from can (do not flatten), and use a 1-inch circle biscuit cutter to cut holes out of the center of each biscuit.

Air fry the donuts for 5 minutes each and air fry the cut-out holes for just 3 minutes.

As each batch of donuts and holes comes out of the fryer, use a pastry brush to paint butter over the entire surface of each donut and hole. After each donut and hole is painted with butter, drop them into the bowl with the sugar mixture and coat completely with the mixture. Gently shake off excess. Serve donuts and holes warm.

Temperature: 375ºF   Time: 15 minutes

BAKED APPLE WITH NUT CRUMBLE

INGREDIENTS

Baked Apple

1 Granny Smith apple

1 tbsp brown sugar

1 tbsp melted butter

Nut Crumble

1 tbsp walnuts, chopped

1 tbsp almonds, chopped

1 tbsp brown sugar

1 tbsp raisins

1 tbsp rolled oats

DIRECTIONS

Using a small paring knife, remove the center of the apple without puncturing the bottom to create a large cavity for the nut crumble. Toss cored apple with brown sugar and melted butter.

In a small bowl, combine walnuts, almonds, brown sugar, raisins, and oats. Pour the nut mixture into the apple cavity and place the apple into your Air Fryer.

Air fry at 375ºF for 15 minutes. Remove and serve with whipped cream, if desired.

Temperature: 400ºF   Time: 15 minutes

APPLE FRIES

INGREDIENTS

1 granny smith apple, peeled, cored, cut into ½" fries

½ tsp ground cinnamon

1 tbsp brown sugar

1 cup all-purpose flour

1 cup maple syrup, honey, or agave nectar

2 cups unsalted, plain breadcrumbs

DIRECTIONS

Toss apple fries with cinnamon and brown sugar. Dredge in flour and shake off any excess. Dip apple fries into maple syrup, then breadcrumbs, and shake off any excess.

Place in the Air Fryer in one layer, careful to avoid overlapping, and separating into 2 batches if necessary.

Air fry at 400°F for 15 minutes, shaking once halfway through. Serve with whipped cream, if desired.

CHEESECAKE

INGREDIENTS

Graham Cracker Crust

¼ cup graham cracker, crumbs

2 tbsp unsalted butter, melted

1 tbsp white sugar

Cheesecake

1 (8oz) package cream cheese, softened

1 tbsp sour cream

½ cup white sugar

1 egg

DIRECTIONS

Combine graham cracker crumbs, butter, and sugar in a small bowl and mix thoroughly to combine. Divide the mixture in half and press into the bases of 2 (4") springform molds.

Cream together the cream cheese, sour cream, and sugar in a mixer. Add egg and let mix until smooth. Divide mixture in half and pour into springform molds.

Air fry for 25-35 minutes, or until a toothpick inserted at the center comes out clean. Remove cheesecake from the Air Fryer and let cool. Transfer the cheesecakes to a sheet tray and place in refrigerator to set for 8 hours or overnight.

Serve chilled with almonds, walnuts, honey, and powdered sugar, if desired.

CHOCOLATE SOUFFLÉ

INGREDIENTS

1 tbsp unsalted butter

2 tbsp white sugar

3 egg yolks

3 egg whites

¼ cup white sugar

¼ cup semisweet chocolate chips, melted

DIRECTIONS

Butter 2 (3") ramekins and dust with sugar. Shake off excess sugar and place in freezer until soufflé batter is ready. Mix egg yolks and half of the sugar in a mixer with a whisk attachment until the egg yolks lighten and ribbons begin to form in the mixture. Add melted chocolate and continue to whisk until combined. Reserve.

In a clean mixing bowl, whip the egg whites and rest of the sugar until soft peaks form. Continue to whip right before the egg whites reach a stiff peak. Take 2 tbsp of egg whites and mix into the chocolate mixture. Gradually add the rest of the egg whites, a little at a time, folding to incorporate. Transfer the soufflé batter to the ramekins, filling halfway. Place the ramekins in the Air Fryer and air fry at 350°F for 10-15 minutes, or until lightly browned and puffy. Serve with powdered sugar and raspberries, if desired.

PRO TIP

You can check the status of your soufflé by gently pulling the Air Fryer door open. Make sure to fill ramekins evenly so you can take out all soufflés at the same time.

Temperature: 400ºF   Time: 10–12 minutes

CINNAMON SUGAR MINI PRETZELS

INGREDIENTS

1 (9") pie crust shell, thawed or pie crust shell scraps, thawed

2 tbsp unsalted butter, melted

2-3 tbsp granulated white sugar

2 tsp ground cinnamon

DIRECTIONS

Separate the softened pie crust into 2" round dough balls. Roll each ball of pie crust into ½" thick cylinders. Fold the ends of the cylinders toward each other so that they form a pretzel shape. Repeat for each ball of pie crust. Pretzels should be 3.5" - 4" at their longest.

Place 3 pretzels into the Air Fryer in one layer. Air fry at 400ºF for 10-12 minutes, or until desired level of crispiness. Carefully remove the pretzels and dip them into melted butter. Combine sugar with cinnamon and stir to incorporate fully. Toss the pretzels in the cinnamon sugar mix and dust off any excess. Serve hot.

PRO TIP

Collect pie crust shell scraps from making Mini Pumpkin Pie or Apple Pie in refrigerator and bring to room temperature to use for Mini Pretzels.

RED VELVET CUPCAKES

INGREDIENTS

½ cup unsalted butter

½ cup sour cream

¾ cup white sugar

2 eggs

1 ¼ cup all-purpose flour

2 tbsp unsweetened cocoa powder

½ tsp kosher salt

½ tsp baking soda

1 oz red food coloring

cupcake liners, double lined

DIRECTIONS

Cream butter, sour cream, and sugar in a mixer until smooth. Add the eggs, one at a time, and mix until incorporated. Whisk together flour, cocoa powder, salt, and baking soda in a separate bowl. Add the flour mixture to the butter mixture slowly, leaving the mixer on throughout the entire process.

When the cupcake batter is thoroughly combined, add the red food coloring. Place 2-3 cupcake liners into the Air Fryer. Dollop approximately 1 tbsp of cupcake batter per cupcake liner. Air fry at 375°F for 12-15 minutes, or until a toothpick inserted into the center comes out clean.

Temperature: 350ºF   Time: 10 minutes

EASY CINNAMON ROLLS
WITH CREAM CHEESE GLAZE

INGREDIENTS

Cinnamon Rolls

4 pieces biscuit dough, can be store-bought

3 tbsp brown sugar

1 tsp ground cinnamon

Cream Cheese Glaze

¼ cup cream cheese

2 tbsp milk, warm

¼ cup powdered sugar

DIRECTIONS

Roll the biscuit dough pieces out into long ovals with a rolling pin. Toss together the brown sugar and ground cinnamon. Dust both sides of the dough ovals with the cinnamon sugar mix.

Roll the ovals into long cylinders. Slice the cylinders into 1" thick rolls. Place the rolls into the Air Fryer and air fry in batches at 350ºF for 10 minutes each until well-browned on top and the centers are cooked through.

Soften the cream cheese in a microwave for 30 seconds. Combine the milk with powdered sugar and whisk until smooth. Add the cream cheese and continue to whisk until combined. Top cinnamon rolls with cream cheese glaze, if desired.

Temperature: 350ºF   Time: 35 minutes

FLOURLESS CHOCOLATE CAKE

INGREDIENTS

10 bananas

10 tsp organic cocoa powder

4 tbsp honey

8 large eggs

1 large avocado

DIRECTIONS

Add all your ingredients (apart from the avocado) to a blender and blend until you have a smooth batter. Place enough to one side for the icing, and divide the rest between two small baking tins. Place the tins in the Air Fryer for 35 minutes at 350°F.

When done, remove the cakes from the tins and allow them to cool on a wire rack. With the rest of the cake mixture, add the avocado until you have a much thicker paste.

Sandwich a small amount in between the two cakes and then use the rest for a chocolate icing around the cake. Place the cake in the fridge for an hour so that the icing can set.

Temperature: 375°F   Time: 15 minutes

MINI PUMPKIN PIE

INGREDIENTS

1 (9") pie crust shell, thawed

3 (3.5") oven-safe ramekins

1 (15 oz) can pumpkin pie purée

DIRECTIONS

Cut out 5-6" diameter circles in a pie crust shell. Transfer the crust circles to ramekins and overlap any edges if necessary to fit the crust into ramekins.

Fill each ramekin up to ¼" below the top with the pumpkin pie purée. Place 1 ramekin in the Air Fryer at a time and air fry for 15 minutes.

OLIVE OIL SPONGE CAKE

INGREDIENTS

1 tbsp unsalted butter

1 tbsp all-purpose flour

½ cup white sugar

3 egg yolks

½ lemon, juiced

1 tsp poppy seed (optional)

⅔ cup all-purpose flour

1 ½ tbsp cornstarch

⅔ cup extra virgin olive oil

3 egg whites

¼ cup white sugar

DIRECTIONS

Butter 2 (4") springform molds and dust with flour. Shake off any excess flour and place in the freezer until sponge cake batter is ready.

Mix egg yolks and ½ cup of sugar in a mixer with a whisk attachment until egg yolks lighten in color significantly and ribbons begin to form in the mixture. Add lemon juice and poppy seeds and continue to whisk to combine. Add flour and cornstarch and whisk to combine. Add olive oil and continue whisking until well combined. Reserve the olive oil mixture.

In a new mixing bowl with a clean whisk attachment, whip the egg whites with sugar until a soft peak forms. Scoop approximately 2 tbsp of egg whites and stir gently into the olive oil mixture. Gradually add the rest of the egg whites, a little a time, folding to incorporate. Transfer the batter to springform molds, filling the molds halfway. Place 1 mold in the Air Fryer and air fry at 400°F for 15-20 minutes, or until lightly browned on top and a toothpick inserted in the center comes out clean. Serve with powdered sugar and strawberries, if desired.

INDEX

ABOUT
THE AUTHORS

CATHERINE-GAIL REINHARD is a passionate cook, fearless foodie and the VP, Product Strategy & Marketing for Dash. She is also the executive editor of the bestselling cookbook *One Pan Kitchen*, now in its second edition, and *One Pot Meals*, a book about hacking your rice cooker. Having grown up in New York and France, she has an equal fondness for baguettes and bagels. She lives in Brooklyn with a tiny kitchen that is filled to the gills with Dash products.

JENNY DORSEY is a professional chef and culinary consultant based in New York and Los Angeles. She is the founder of Wednesdays, a tasting restaurant combining fine dining with intellectually stimulating conversation. Jenny's food and work have been featured in publications such as *Harper's Bazaar*, *Business Insider*, *Thrillist*, *The Huffington Post*, *7x7*, *Village Voice*, as well as on Food Network and Oxygen TV. She lives in Hudson with her two dogs and one husband.